The Color Nature Library
SMALL ANIMALS

By
JANE BURTON

Designed by
DAVID GIBBON

Produced by
TED SMART

CRESCENT BOOKS

First published in Great Britain 1977 by Colour Library International Ltd.
Designed by David Gibbon. Produced by Ted Smart.
© Text: Jane Burton. © Illustrations: Jane Burton/Bruce Coleman Ltd.
Colour separations by La Cromolito, Milan, Italy.
Display and Text filmsetting by Focus Photoset, London, England.
Printed and bound by L.E.G.O. Vicenza, Italy.
Published by Crescent Books, a division of Crown Publishers Inc.
Library of Congress Catalogue Card No. 77-18623
CRESCENT 1978

Introduction

Traditionally, the word 'animal' meant any warm-blooded furred beast that suckled its young– that is, not a bird or a cold-blooded creature. But when people began to study the living world more seriously than before and the science of zoology was born, it became necessary to distinguish the sections of the animal kingdom more precisely. So the furry suckling animals were classed as *mammals* whereas the term *animal* was taken to mean any member of the animal kingdom, from a single-celled amoeba to the mighty Blue Whale, or any worm, insect, fish, frog, snake or bird in between. But in everyday speech we still tend to call a mammal by its traditional name, animal.

This book, then, is strictly-speaking about small mammals. But how small is 'small'? To a scientist studying small mammals it means anything the size of a rat or smaller. However, this is still a rather vague definition, because there are many sizes of rat, some almost mouse-sized, others as big as a small cat. So I have taken 'small animals' to include any mammal from the size of a small domestic cat down to the tiniest mammal. This covers a whole host of creatures, mainly rodents, bats and insectivores, but also the smallest monkeys, fox and otters, as well as other small carnivores such as the Stoat and Dwarf Mongoose. The largest rat included is the Giant or Pouched Rat of Africa, and the smallest mouse, the European Harvest Mouse. The smallest mammals in the world are the Pygmy Shrews of Europe and the United States which are so small they can travel in the tunnels of large beetles. Harvest Mice are only slightly larger.

Of all mammals, small or large, by far the most numerous both in numbers of species as well as in numbers of individuals, are the rodents. There are over sixteen hundred different kinds, including not only rats and mice, but squirrels, hamsters, voles, lemmings, gerbils. (Rabbits and hares were at one time classed as rodents, but because their teeth differ in important respects from those of rats, squirrels and so on, they are now classed separately).

Rodents can be found all over the land in almost every kind of habitat from the sea-shore to the snow-line of mountains, in deserts, grassy plains or forests, in cities, farms and gardens, underground, all over the ground, and in bushes and trees. Unfortunately, a few destructive kinds have given the order a bad name, but for every pest there are a score or more of harmless and inoffensive species living obscure but complex lives, influencing their environment in small or drastic ways, eating plants and preying on smaller animals, and themselves occasionally being eaten by larger animals. A few kinds of rodents may be scourges of the human race, hated as destructive carriers of diseases; but others have been domesticated and make invaluable laboratory animals as well as much-loved pets. Small wonder, then, that rodents appear more frequently than other kinds of small animals in the following pages.

Page 1   A Bank Vole climbing among rose hips.

Page 2-3   A Common Rat running along a farm fence is silhouetted against the setting sun.

Polecats *left* are very playful animals, and both the adults and young have much fun tumbling together and chasing one another. Play helps young animals sharpen their wits and strengthen their muscles. Adults particularly play together during courtship, and also spend much time grooming one another, nibbling and licking around the neck and back of the head. Such mutual grooming helps to strengthen the bond between two animals.

Harvest Mice

The Harvest Mouse is one of the smallest mammals. It lives among the long grasses and rank vegetation of ditches and hedgerows, in dry reed beds and in fields of oats and wheat *left*. It spends much of its waking time climbing to feed on seeds and insects. Like other climbing mice and rats, its hind feet are hand-like; the outer toe is opposable and gives a firm grasp on thin stems. All the time the Harvest Mouse is climbing, its tail wraps loosely around the stalk or leaves behind it; even around its mate's tail *centre right*. When the mouse stops, the tail tip holds on tight like a fifth hand. Firmly anchored by its hind feet and tail the mouse then has its front paws free for feeding *top right* or it can stretch out as far as it can reach to satisfy its curiosity *bottom right*.

Harvest mice are active by day and night. Like other very small mammals they have a three-hourly rhythm, alternately sleeping and feeding through the 24 hours. They sleep for perhaps 1½ to 2 hours, feed for half an hour, and spend the rest of the time grooming themselves, exploring and nest making. In summer the female makes a breeding nest of split and shredded grass blades or wheat leaves, spherical and about the size of a tennis ball, strung low down between upright stems. The winter nest is in a burrow in the ground or in a rick of hay or straw, and is just a heap of shredded grasses. Neither nest has a proper entrance hole like a bird's nest would have; the mice just dive in and pull the bedclothes together behind them..

All the mice pictured here are Old World Harvest Mice. This species can be found right across Europe from Britain to Siberia and China. There is also an American Harvest Mouse, but it is quite unrelated to the Old World Harvest Mouse. The two harvest mice are about the same size and have come to look alike because they live in the same type of habitat and have the same climbing habits. The main external difference is that the tail of the American Harvest Mouse is not prehensile.

Unfortunately, these pretty and in-offensive little mice are much less common today than they used to be. Mechanised harvesting and the burning of stubble make wheat fields uncomfortable places for small animals to live in.

A Mouse in the House

Mice have been sharing our homes for at least six thousand years, in fact probably ever since we first stopped being wandering hunters and settled down to agriculture. The first mouse to become intimately associated with man was the House Mouse, no doubt because its wild ancestors happened to be living in the right place at the right time. It was admirably suited to take advantage of the association, for it was small, agile and alert, nocturnal and with a high rate of reproduction. It can live on all kinds of food and survive for long periods without drinking. So successfully did it adapt to domestic conditions that it was carried all over the world, from the steppes of Central Asia where it began the association, to the Middle East, the Mediterranean lands and thence through the whole of northern Europe. From Europe it spread to North America, India, Australia and Africa. In most places it is an indoor animal, but where the climate is mild it breeds out of doors as

well. For instance, in the West Indies it can be seen foraging on the drift-line along the beach *top left* living on water-borne seeds, coconuts and chunks of discarded sugar cane.

In various parts of the world other kinds of mice take advantage of the benefits of human homes, but have not become established as permanent commensals. One of the most delightful of occasional visitors is the tiny African Dormouse *top right* grey, mouse-sized and nocturnal but with a fluffy squirrel-like tail. It feeds mainly on insects, and is attracted to the feast of moths and winged termites that fly into lighted rooms at night. During periods when flying insects are less abundant, it can find something to subsist on among the table scraps.

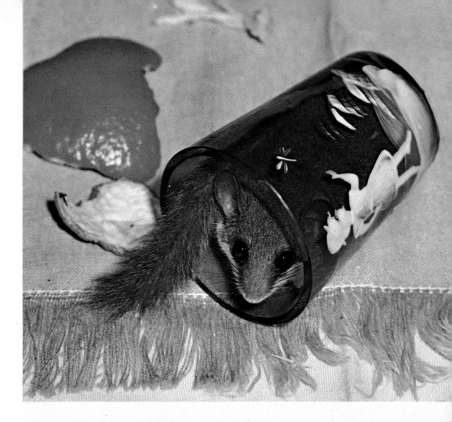

The Spiny Mouse *bottom left* comes into houses during the winter in North Africa and some Mediterranean countries. In Roman times it foraged among strewn rushes on the floor by the light of a lamp fuelled with olive oil, just as today it picks up crumbs from the carpets of houses lit by electricity. Away from human habitations it lives among rocks in semi-desert places.

The West African Pygmy Mouse *bottom right* is another of the world's smallest mammals. It is related to the House Mouse, and like it can live almost anywhere, in holes, among thick vegetation, or in houses where, because it is so small, it often forages unnoticed. These three young Pygmy Mice are after the cooked rice in a small calabash bowl.

Overground

One of the best-loved and most familiar rodents is the Golden Hamster, but there are a dozen other species of hamster ranging from the fierce guinea pig-sized Common Hamster of Europe down to the tiny gentle Dwarf Hamster of Siberia. Hamsters live in dry places, on the borders of deserts, among sand dunes or on steppes. They are not climbing animals, and do not jump; they are built for swarming at speed over and under and among rocks and logs and along the ground. They all have cheek pouches, built-in hold-alls into which they cram enormous amounts of food or nesting material.

The Golden Hamster *bottom left and top right* is almost unknown in the wild. A single specimen was found at Aleppo in Syria in 1839, but nothing was seen of the animal again until 1930 when a female with twelve young was dug up and captured alive. From two females and a male of this litter come all the Golden Hamsters in our homes today. They make ideal pets, clean and tidy, amusing in their ways, and tame when handled frequently. Their only disadvantage is their nocturnal habits. Females give birth to 6-12 young which are weaned at about a month old and soon go their own ways, for Golden Hamsters are solitary animals.

The Chinese Hamster *top centre and bottom right* is also a solitary animal. Males and females come together only for mating; if the male cannot escape soon afterwards the female may kill him. Chinese Hamsters are smaller than the Golden and have a longer tail. They too make interesting and delightful pets.

Prettiest and most gentle of hamsters is the Dwarf Hamster *top left*. Males and females live amicably together and allow their families to live with them. They are easily tamed because even wild ones do not attempt to defend themselves by biting. They eat all kinds of seeds and other plant material, and also beetle grubs and other insect food. Dwarf Hamsters are very unusual among rodents in that in the wild they turn white in winter.

Curiosity

A sense of curiosity is common to all animals. They need to know what is going on around them. Curiosity is linked with the search for food and escape from enemies, but needs to be satisfied for its own sake also. Curiosity killed the cat and satisfaction brought it back. The same is true of the rat, the gerbil, the shrew and most of the rest of the animal kingdom.

The Brown Rat *left* is a very wary animal; anything new is investigated from a distance first, by the nose chiefly, the rat standing up to get as clear a scent picture as possible.

Gerbils are desert animals that come out at night to search for seeds or insects, and anything unusual must be investigated. This female Small Naked-soled Gerbil of East Africa *top right* with one of her babies watching, is sniffing a large Jewel Beetle, which tucks its head down in its defensive posture. She does not find it edible; its stony wing cases and tough skin form too hard a nut for small rodent teeth to crack.

The Common Shrew *middle right* lives in a world so different from ours it is hard for us to comprehend. It is a world mainly of scents and very high-pitched sounds which we are unable to detect. Our world is one of sights, but the shrew has tiny eyes and lives in a dim world where only light and dark can be distinguished, certainly no colours. The shrew therefore investigates its world by smell and taste. Chancing upon a snail with eye-stalks extended, it gives one a nip to test edibility. The snail withdraws smartly into its shell, but the shrew does not attempt to extract it, presumably finding from the one taste that it is unpalatable.

The Giant or Pouched Rat *bottom right* is a very large rat found throughout Africa. In spite of its size, it is not aggressive; in fact, it is a gentle and inoffensive beast, though occasionally causing damage to crops such as cocoa. Here it investigates newly-harvested pods. It may gnaw one open and lick the sweet mucilage from the beans. Its pouches are cheek pockets in which it can carry extra food for storage in its burrow.

13

Eyes at Night

Most small mammals live in a world of smells and sounds, rather than sights, but nocturnal mammals generally have large eyes and can probably see better in the dark than we can. To help them make the most of small amounts of light, they have a tapetum behind the retina of the eye. This is a layer of silvery crystals which acts as a reflector. In an ordinary eye, much of the light that enters it passes between the light-receptive cells of the retina and is absorbed in the tissues behind, but a tapetum reflects some of that lost light back so that it passes twice through the retina and has a double chance of striking the receptor cells. A nocturnal animal with a tapetum is therefore able to use 50 per cent more of the available light, and so can see very much better than we can in the dark.

It is an exciting experience to go out at night and search for small animals with a torch. The light must be held fairly close to one's own eyes so that one is looking along its beam. The eyes of any animal with a tapetum then appear as twin reflectors. If the animal turns its head, the lights go out. If it moves its eyes, the colour of the reflection can change from yellow to red or green; it can even appear to have one green eye and one red, or one yellow and one green. The photographer's flashlight is also reflected brilliantly.

The Common Genet *top left* is a nocturnal cat-like animal that hunts roosting birds, tree rats and other small prey in the trees at night. It is found throughout southern Africa as well as Spain and southern France. Like a cat, its eyes stop down to vertical slits during the day.

The Senegal Bushbaby *bottom left* also lives in Africa. It is a kind of nocturnal primate; like a monkey its eyes are directed forward to give stereoscopic vision, important to an arboreal animal that needs to judge distance exactly. It has very long hind legs which give it great springing power. At night it leaps from branch to branch with great agility, searching for insects and acacia gum.

Opossums are the only marsupials that live outside Australia. This Murine or Mouse Opossum *top right* was photographed in a Jamaica plum tree on the West Indian island of Grenada. Its eyes are relatively large and bright-looking, but like a mouse's eyes are probably very short-sighted. Here the flashlight

was too far to the side to reflect on the animal's tapetum. This opossum is a fierce little beast, and puts on a good show in self-defence. The tail is prehensile, to help in climbing; when not in use it can be coiled like a chameleon's. Females give birth to about a dozen tiny young, born, like all marsupials, after a very short gestation and at an early stage of development. In spite of their immaturity these babies make their own way into their mother's pouch where they attach themselves to her nipples and remain for another ten weeks until weaned.

The Brown Hare *bottom right* has large protruding eyes set on the sides of the head in a fixed stare. It has no need to move its eyes or its head to look around; it can see forwards, backwards and upwards at the same time as sideways. The bright light reflected from one eye must have been very dazzling and confusing for this hare, but its other eye probably continued to function well in the dark as it lolloped away.

Ultrasounds

It is well-known that bats navigate by means of echo-location. The Pipistrelle *above* emits high-pitched squeaks through the mouth. (To avoid deafening itself it closes off the ears simultaneously). The sound bounces back off objects and from the time it takes to return the bat can tell how far away an object is. Leaf-nosed bats such as the Horseshoe Bat *bottom left* emit squeaks through the nose in a narrow beam. Both sonar systems are so sensitive and accurate that bats can flit among fine wires without touching them, and catch tiny insects on the wing.

It is now being realised that many kinds of small animals use ultrasounds. The young of many rodents such as the Greater Egyptian Gerbil *top left* emit ultrasonic squeaks when uncomfortable, which the mother instantly responds to. The Common Shrew *right*, an animal that prefers its own company, has high-pitched shrieking contests with anyone else that invades its privacy.

Big-ears

"Granny, what big ears you've got," said Little Red Riding Hood. "All the better to hear you with" was the wolf's reply.

There is no doubt that big ears, such as those of the European Rabbit *left* are reflectors for collecting sound. The Long-eared Bat *above* is a tiny animal with enormous ears for its size and ultra-sensitive hearing. Probably as finely-tuned are the ears of some small nocturnal desert rodents; they have hearing so sensitive they can detect the minute sounds made by a striking snake or owl and can leap aside in a split second to escape. The large ears of the King Gerbil *top right* are very efficient sound-collectors, but as an added bonus they act as radiators, giving off heat and keeping the animal cool. Many other desert animals such as the Fennec *right* have exceptionally big ears to help them keep cool. The Fennec is the smallest kind of fox but it has the largest ears.

In the Air

Bats are the only mammals that can really fly. They are almost exclusively nocturnal, so have the night air almost to themselves since most birds are diurnal. There are two main categories of bats: the insect-eaters, which are mostly small; and the fruit bats, rather bigger animals with large eyes and good night vision.

Fruit bats may congregate in enormous numbers to roost by day in caves or in trees. These are Dog-faced Fruit Bats *top right* in Batu Caves, Malaya.

The Epauletted Fruit Bat of Africa *bottom right* hangs upside down to feed on wild figs or other ripening fruit. It chews each mouthful to extract the juice, then spits out a pellet of dry fibres.

The Jamaican Fruit-eating Bat *left* is not a true fruit bat but its teeth have become adapted to a diet of fruit instead of insects.

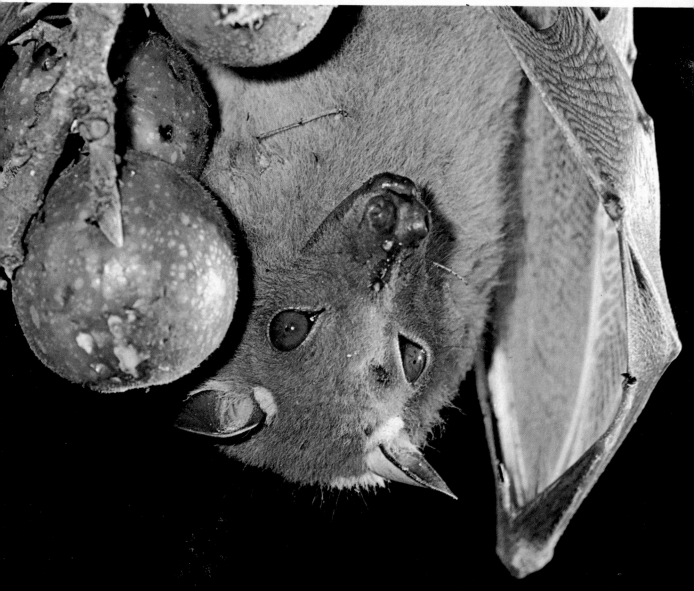

Communication

Animals communicate with one another in a variety of ways. Those with quite good eyesight use visual signals, supplemented by sounds and smells. When the Scottish Wild Cat is peaceful and unprovoked it looks as gentle as a fireside puss. Its ears are erect, its eyes almond-shaped, its mouth closed and its whiskers alert but not bristling *top left*. But when two males dispute territory or a cornered wild cat faces a larger predator, its appearance changes completely. Its ears are pulled down, its eyes round, its teeth bare and it spits and snarls, a demon of ferocity *bottom left*.

Animals that live together must have a means of keeping in touch when the colony is scattered. Mongolian Gerbils *top centre* maintain contact by drumming rhythmically on the ground with their hind feet.

The Tree Hyrax *top right* keeps in touch with its neighbours in the African high forests by letting out a series of blood-curdling screams at dead of night. Other Tree Hyraxes all around take up the chorus.

The African Bush Squirrel *bottom right* is constantly alert to the threat of aerial attack from eagles and hawks. If it spots a bird of prey overhead it flags its tail and gives an alarm call which monkeys and birds, as well as other squirrels, respond to.

Underground

The Springhare *top left* has the largest ears of any rodent. This extraordinary animal lives in the grasslands of Africa south of the Sahara and looks like a cross between a kangaroo and a rabbit. By day it lives in a large warren of underground burrows shared by many springhares but each sleeping in its own bedroom. At night it comes out and bounds along on its big hind feet, dropping onto all fours when grazing. Its long ears help it to remain cool by dissipating excess body heat, but when the night becomes cold it can fold its ears down to avoid too much cooling. To keep out sand when digging, it has a tragus or earlet with which it can close the ear.

Animals that live in hot deserts need underground burrows not only as a safe refuge from enemies, but also to escape from the rigours of the climate. Small mammals cannot cool themselves by sweating and panting, because they would lose too much body moisture and die from dehydration. They therefore spend the heat of the day in relatively cool and damp underground burrows, and, like the Dwarf Gerbil *top right*, only come out to forage when the sun has gone down.

Life underground is relatively secure and stable, so several different kinds of animals have become adapted to a permanent subterranean existence. The European Mole *bottom right* is the underground animal *par excellence*. Its whole skeleton and body shape are perfectly adapted for tunnelling through soft earth: its hands have become combined shovel-and-picks located each side of a sensitive worm-detecting snout; it has small eyes and ears hidden in the soft short fur which can be brushed backwards without discomfort to the wearer. Its main food is earthworms, which it holds down and pulls through its hands while eating, to scrape off loose earth and worm slime. It also eats leatherjackets and wire-worms. A single mole may eat 80lb of worms and grubs in a year.

Moles are not the only underground mammals; nearly a hundred different species of rodents live a burrowing existence. Some come to the surface to feed, but others are nearly as special-ised as a mole for an entirely underground life. Among these is the Kenya Mole Rat *bottom left*. Its hands are more multi-purpose than those of the mole, and it digs more like a rabbit than a plough. But it too has soft dense fur, and small ears and eyes. It feeds on roots, succulent bulbs and tubers, which it demolishes with its enormous orange incisors. These are also used to loosen stones and chop through roots. Very occasionally a small stone may get wedged between the teeth, as has happened to this Mole Rat. The teeth are pushed apart so that the cutting edges of upper and lower pairs no longer meet and one of the incisors, which are growing continuously, is not kept worn down but grows out in a curve. The rat is unable to dig or feed properly and will starve. In this case the animal was rescued; the stone was removed and the overgrown tooth cut.

In the Trees

Many kinds of mice and rats can climb very well without being particularly specialised for life in the trees. They have multi-purpose feet as good at grasping twigs as at running along the ground. Their other main requirement for climbing is a long tail which can be held out or swung rapidly as a balancer, or wrapped around twigs for support.

The European Long-tailed Field Mouse *left* lives in woods, hedgerows and gardens, making runways under leaf-litter and tunnels underground. It forages mainly at night, looking for nuts, seeds and berries, which it may hoard in large stores, in hollow logs, holes in the ground, even in old birds' nests. Such stores are often thought to be the work of a squirrel, but squirrels hide their nuts singly.

The Long-tailed Thicket Rat of Africa *top right* has an exceptionally long tail. It is a very agile climber after fruit and insects, and lives in forests or what has taken the place of the forest. These two Thicket Rats are eating kei apples in a garden hedge.

Another climbing African rat is the Rusty-nosed *centre right*. The climbing forest rats tend to be gentle and un-aggressive, but highly strung. If their nest is aloft they must be alert for high winds and storms. They are also at risk from tree snakes and climbing carni-vores like the genet, though twigs and leaves shield them from swooping birds of prey.

The Acacia Rat *bottom right* makes a big nest of spiky twigs in the top of a thorn tree. In the African savannah small flat-topped thorn trees grow close together and the rats can forage from tree to tree without coming down to the ground; but if disturbed in their nest they hurtle to the ground to find a better hiding place there. When a mother Acacia Rat with a young brood is frightened out of the nest, she carries her babies with her still sucking tight onto her teats, enabling the whole family to escape together.

Monkeys and their Kin

Monkeys are our little cousins. There are many kinds, and nearly all live in warm countries, in the trees, in forest or jungle, and go about in troops feeding on fruit, leaves and insects. Their hands are like ours, but their feet are also hand-like because their big toe is like a thumb. This makes them very agile at climbing. They also pick up their food with their hands, unlike squirrels and mice who usually first pick up the food in the mouth and then transfer it to the front paws for holding while they eat.

Monkey's faces are much like ours and they are very expressive. They communicate with each other with signs which include scowling and grinning. They also have sound languages of many different calls. They have good eyesight, which they must have for a life in the trees. They also have colour vision like us, and many have colourful or strikingly-patterned coats.

The squirrel-sized Squirrel Monkey *top left* lives in large troops in the edges of South American jungles. Its food is fruit, buds and insects found in the tops of trees or on the ground. Some South American monkeys have a prehensile tail almost as efficient as a fifth hand, but the Squirrel Monkey's long tail is used as a counterbalance or looped loosely round a branch for extra support.

The Spot-nosed Monkey *bottom left* lives in the forests of West Africa. There are several different kinds of white-nosed monkeys; this one has a neat, heart-shaped spot, others have a diamond-shaped mark. Other related species in the same forests have white eyebrows or cheek tufts or moustaches. Such distinctive facial markings make it easy for monkeys to recognise their own kind over a distance or among dark foliage.

Marmosets are the smallest of all monkeys and live in South America. The Black-plumed *top right* is tiny, a pygmy of the monkey world; but some species are even smaller. Marmosets are very active, bounding through the trees with jerky, squirrel-like movements. Also squirrel-like are the tufts of whiskers on the wrist which help them feel handholds.

The Slow Loris *middle right* is a monkey relative that creeps stealthily among the branches of Malaysian forests. Unlike monkeys it is entirely nocturnal, sleeping by day rolled into a ball and coming out at night to feed on fruit or any small insect, bird, or reptile which it can creep up on and catch with a final lightning pounce of a paw. Females carry their single or twin babies clinging to their fur.

The Tree Shrew of South-east Asia *bottom right* is a most extraordinary little animal. It is not a shrew though it has some shrew-like characteristics and eats insects; and it does not live in trees though it climbs bushes with great agility. Squirrel-like in some ways, it is active, inquisitive and intelligent. But in spite of its rodent-like appearance it is thought to be related to monkeys and ourselves—a living representative of the most primitive primate stock from which the monkeys and we evolved millions of years ago.

29

Squirrels

Most squirrels are tree-dwelling animals, active by day. They have long legs for leaping, long flexible fingers and toes for grasping twigs, and long claws for getting a grip on bark. The plumed tail, like that of the Grey Squirrel *left*, acts as a counterbalance and can also be used as a parachute when leaping and as a blanket to tuck around itself when the squirrel goes to sleep.

Not all squirrels live in trees. Where forests have disappeared, squirrels have adapted to a terrestrial life. A Ground Squirrel *top right* habitually stands up on its hind legs when feeding, to keep a better watch out over its barren terrain.

One of the most brightly-coloured rodents is the Red Squirrel *bottom right*. Squirrels have good vision–they need it for travelling at speed through the tree-tops–but it is doubtful if they can appreciate colours.

Spots and Stripes

The usual colour of rodent fur is a nondescript speckled brown or grey which blends well with almost any background: plain-coloured little animals are usually very secretive and keep well out of sight in thick cover. Rodents are generally nocturnal and when alarmed dash back to the safety of their burrows along well-worn runs which they know like the back of their paws.

A few small rodents have quite brightly-coloured spotted or striped coats. When these animals are moving about, they are quite conspicuous, but when alarmed they 'freeze', pressing the body to the ground or to a branch and blending into the background. Several kinds of squirrels, such as the North American chipmunks and the African and Indian palm squirrels are boldly striped, and three kinds of African rats are strikingly marked with spots or stripes. Both the squirrels and the striped rats are active in the daytime and live in woods or among grass around the edges and clearings of forests. Their brightly-patterned coats blend with the dappled sunlight and shadows, and help to break up the outlines of the body, so concealing them from hawks and eagles that hunt by eyesight in the daytime. (No cryptic colouring could hide the nocturnal rodents from owls that find their prey in the dark mainly by means of very acute hearing).

The Zebra Mouse or Striped Grass Mouse is a very pretty mouse or small rat. Its fur is mostly a speckled brown, with longitudinal light and dark stripes down the spine. Alert and active, it feeds by day on a wide variety of seeds, berries and buds, and has unusually good eyesight for a mouse. Found only in Africa, it is common on the high plateaux where it lives in grassy areas between forests and on agricultural land. The Zebra Mouse makes its nest of shredded grasses, leaves and moss in a clump of grass or in a shallow burrow. There are usually five or six babies to a litter and like most mice they are born naked, blind and helpless. But they are already clearly striped at birth, the stripes marked by dark pigment in the otherwise pinkish skin *top left*. The babies' eyes open on about the third day. They begin to groom their new stripy fur, and at about two weeks of age they are lively and active, venturing from the nest in search of solid food *bottom left*.

The Spotted Grass Mouse *right* is another very pretty little animal, slightly larger than the Zebra Mouse. It has a much wider geographical range and is also a diurnal seed-eater. Despite its name, the Spotted Grass Mouse appears to be striped, buff on a dark background; the stripes are made up of a series of closely-placed spots.

The chipmunk *below* is a small ground squirrel that lives in woods. There are two kinds, the Eastern Chipmunk and the Western. They are good climbers but prefer to stay on the ground. They also busy themselves underground, digging long and complicated systems of burrows under rocks and fallen logs. They feed on berries, fruits, buds and seeds that have fallen to the ground. Like hamsters and the Pouched Rat, they can harvest and carry off in their cheek pouches extra food for underground storage. Their dark and light body stripes extend down the sides of the head, one dark stripe running through the eye to mask it and aid in concealing the shape of the animal when it 'freezes'.

Water Animals

No small mammals are truly aquatic. The only fully aquatic mammals are all large – the whales, dugong and manatees. Seals, sealions and sea otters come on land to give birth. However, many small mammals have discovered the advantages of living beside water, which provides food and instant escape. Quite a few rodents and insectivores have become amphibious; some, such as the Otter Shrew and some fish-eating rats of South America have webbed feet for swimming and closable ears to keep out the water. Most of these specialised swimmers live along mountain streams in tropical countries, and are extremely rare. But around European waterways there are two much more familiar animals, less specialised but quite common.

The Water Vole *top left* lives beside lakes and rivers, nesting in burrows in the bank and feeding on the lush waterside vegetation. It is the largest sort of native European vole, thickset, with small rounded ears and dense waterproof fur. Sometimes called the Water Rat, this leads to confusion between it and the Brown Rat, which also often lives along river banks and can dive and swim with similar ease. The Water Vole is very short-sighted, so that it can be approached quite closely from downwind. After all, it does not need marvellous eye-sight, since it can disappear almost instantaneously and swim away underwater when alarmed *top right*.

There are several different species of Water Shrew whose ranges cover all Europe, much of Asia and North America. The fur is almost black on the back and white on the belly. The European species lives not only alongside streams and lakes, but around sea lochs and along the coast, and hunts small creatures such as sand hoppers among the pebbles and seaweed *bottom left*. Its tail has a keel of hairs which makes it a more efficient rudder, and the toes have stiff hairs which turn the paws into paddles. When the shrew swims under-water it looks like an animated silvery bubble due to the air trapped in its fur *bottom right*.

Just as some rodents and insectivores have found the water a favourable habitat, so some members of the weasel tribe have become specialised swimmers. The most aquatic are the otters of which there are several species in various parts of the world. The largest, the Giant Brazilian Otter, can grow longer than a man; the smallest, the Oriental Small-clawed Otter, is smaller than a cat. All otters are much alike in shape and habits. They are long-bodied short-legged animals, with very small ears, a broad muzzle and bristling whiskers helpful for feeling their way or prey in murky water. The stout tapering tail acts as a rudder, and the big hind feet are webbed. The fur is waterproof; there is a thick underfur and only the outer guard hairs become wet and spiky from immersion. Otters live mainly in rivers and lakes, and feed on crayfish, mussels, frogs and water birds, as well as fish.

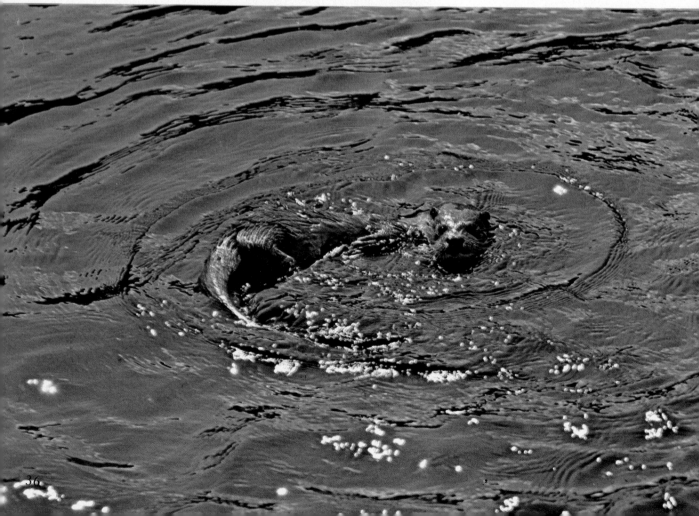

The Asiatic Small-clawed Otter *top left* finds its prey mainly by feeling with its sensitive front paws under pebbles and among mud and roots in shallow water. It has an extremely delicate sense of touch, and can locate and catch freshwater prawns, frogs, river crabs, shellfish and so on, with its fingers. This delightful little otter is easily tamed, and is sometimes kept by fishermen and trained to hunt for them.

The Common Otter *bottom left* is a wonderfully skilful swimmer and very playful, diving after a small pebble or other object, rolling and splashing with it at the surface, tossing it and porpoising after it to catch it before it sinks again. Young otters swim naturally, although they may need to be coaxed or pushed in by their mother before daring to take their first plunge.

Like otters, mink hunt in the water and are rarely seen, being mainly nocturnal. Mink are not so aquatic as otters, although they swim well and live along the banks of streams, rivers and lakes. They also hunt on land like their cousins the stoats and weasels.

There are two species of Mink, the American and the European, both looking much alike. Wild mink can be light or dark brown, but always with a distinctive white patch on the chin *top right*. The mink is one of the most valuable fur-bearing animals, and is farmed extensively for the fur. Many beautiful colours such as the Silver Mink *bottom right* have been bred in captivity. Being strong and resourceful small animals, mink have managed to escape from ranches all over the world and have established themselves in the wild where they were never found previously, including in many parts of Britain, where they are often mistaken for small otters.

Grooming

Grooming is an essential part of the daily routine of most small mammals. It keeps the fur clean and tidy and polishes up barer skin such as ears, paws and tail. Grooming also adds to the physical and mental welfare of an animal and plays a part in courtship and in birth and rearing of the young.

When a baby mammal is born, the mother has a very strong instinct to lick it. This clears the baby's nostrils, and dries its skin and fur. As the young grow, they return the maternal licking. A weanling Small Naked-soled Gerbil is responding to its mother's grooming *top left*. Male and female animals also groom each other especially during courtship; mutual grooming makes the bond between two animals more firm.

A European Rabbit *top centre* nibbles the caked snow off its hind foot. A grooming rabbit also washes its ears, licking its paws, rubbing them over the ears, then licking its paws again. Natural oils on the ears make vitamin D in the sunshine, and while grooming the rabbit swallows these. A young rabbit deprived of sunlight may develop rickets.

Grooming also has a therapeutic effect on a small animal such as the Long-tailed Field Mouse *top right*. By stimulating the blood-flow it induces a feeling of well-being. After a fright, a mouse will groom itself to calm its nerves, as well as rearrange its fur.

A young Egyptian Spiny Mouse grooms its tail *bottom left*. The spines of these mice are not as prickly as a hedgehog's, although sharp enough to make an uncomfortable meal for a snake. Spiny Mice lick their prickles just as other mice lick their fur, but a hedgehog, perhaps wisely, hardly grooms itself at all.

Some other small mammals seem to groom themselves only rarely; guinea pigs and shrews mostly just scratch with a hind foot. A Bank Vole *bottom right* uses its claws to ease a tickle, but usually washes the foot afterwards.

Feeding

The majority of rodents are seed-eaters or general feeders, able to take advantage of whatever food is available, from seeds and fruit to insects, worms and spiders.

The Deer Mouse *left* lives in North America. There are over fifty different species of deer mice, found from Alaska and Labrador southwards, and they live in all sorts of country from swamps to near-deserts. Seeds and berries are their main food, but they will also eat insects. Their diet may change according to what is available at the time of year: one species feeds on seeds in the winter and on butterfly and moth caterpillars in the summer.

The Grey Squirrel *top right* is also a native of North America, but since its introduction into England has become very common there too. It has a special technique for neatly and quickly cracking a hazel nut to extract the kernel. With its sharp incisors it slices off the top of the nut, works a tooth into the crack and splits the shell into halves. Young squirrels do not know how to manage this by instinct and make a mess of their first nuts. In autumn squirrels collect large numbers of nuts, beech mast and acorns but do not store them all in one place. They bury each item singly in a hole in the ground, raking earth and leaves over to hide the place. Later they may find the nut again by smell; but any buried seeds that are not retrieved and eaten will germinate in the spring. Squirrels are thus great assistant foresters, helping to spread and sow tree seeds far from the parent tree.

The little Three-striped Rat *bottom right* lives in the high forests of West Africa. It is grey-brown with a black stripe down the back and a paler stripe on each side. It runs about by day among the leaf litter, feeding on fallen fruits, seeds and insects. Its jerky movements and its disruptive coloration make it very hard to follow, no doubt confusing and thwarting would-be predators. Indeed it is often easier to hear than to see this small animal, as it skitters among the leaves in the otherwise silent forest. Even its tiny teeth make quite a lot of noise as it crunches up a crisp grasshopper.

Grass-eaters

Some rodents that live in grasslands have become specialised for feeding on grasses. This food has the advantage of growing all around, so the animals do not have to search for it, but it has the disadvantage of being tough on the teeth, hard to digest and rather poor in nourishment so that large quantities of it must be consumed to make a decent meal. Some small animals have to eat three times their own weight of grass every two days, and so must spend most of their lives eating. They have special cheek teeth with rasp-like surfaces to shred up the grass, and digestion is aided by special bacteria in the gut. Also, to extract the maximum nourishment from such unpromising food, it is passed twice through the digestive system, not by regurgitation like a cow chewing the cud but by eating their own droppings. After the food's first passage through the system the droppings are soft and rich in vitamin B: the second time, they emerge hard and fairly dry, the valuable vitamins and water extracted.

The chief grazers in northern countries are the voles and lemmings. The tiny Steppe Lemming *left* lives on the arid steppes of Russia and Siberia. Like other grass-eaters it makes a complicated network of runs and tunnels through the grass from which it scarcely ever emerges. It therefore has no need for acute eyesight or hearing, so its eyes are not large and its ears are small and neat against the head. Like many grass-eaters its fur is a nondescript brown, but with a dark stripe down the spine.

The African Grass Rat *top right* is a medium-sized rat very abundant in the grasslands of Africa south of the Sahara. Like other grazers it must eat during the day as well as at night. This is a youngster just out of the nest and experimenting with a grass stem. He was not born with the cellulose-digesting bacteria already in his gut and without these micro-organisms he cannot digest the grass, so he will have obtained a culture by licking his mother soon after birth.

In South America guinea pigs are the major grass-eaters. There are twenty species of wild guinea pigs known as Cuis *bottom right* – pronounced 'kweess,' after their call, which we mimic as 'squeak'. Most grass-eaters have little use for a tail as a balancer or fifth hand, since normally they do no climbing. Voles and lemmings therefore have rather short tails, but guinea pigs have dispensed with tails entirely.

43

A Compulsive Hoarder

Food in the desert is nearly always difficult to find, often it is non-existent. Many desert animals therefore gather up as much food as they can in any short season of plenty and store it in burrows underground to tide them over hard times. The Golden Hamster is the most compulsive desert hoarder of all. To help it carry the maximum of food with the minimum of effort it has capacious cheek pouches into which it can cram an almost incredible number of nuts, seeds or leaves. It therefore needs to be above ground only long enough to actually find the seeds and pouch them. One journey takes the place of many, conserving energy and minimising the risk of attack from predators. Even in captivity, when fresh food is given daily, the hamster has to gather every particle up and transport it to a storage place of its own choosing, usually close to its nest.

Bamboo Dwellers

Bamboo is a kind of giant grass which grows in huge clumps and thickets. As a habitat for small animals it is not very hospitable; the leaves are tough, and little grows on the ground among the stems but small ferns and herbs. However, the new shoots are succulent, as are the roots, which are eaten by burrowing rats; and the hard, hollow stems can provide secure homes for very small animals. Since the world is crowded with a host of different species, it is not surprising that a few small mammals have opted for living in some of the less-favoured places such as among bamboo where the competition is not so intense.

In the bamboo jungles of South-east Asia lives the Pencil-tailed Tree Mouse *top left* (its 'pencil' is a pointed brush of black hairs to the tip of the tail). It makes its home inside a bamboo by gnawing a neat hole in the stem, then gnawing through several of the partitions inside, thus giving itself a house of as many draught free rooms as it needs.

The tiny Malaysian Bamboo Bat *bottom left* is amongst the smallest of bats. It is remarkably adapted for roosting inside hollow bamboo stems; its whole body, and particularly its skull, is flattened. It is so small and flat that it can crawl in and out through narrow slits in split old bamboo stems. In addition, its thumbs and hind feet have special suction pads on them, so that it can cling to the smooth stems and hang up inside them to roost. As many as a dozen of these tiny flat bats may roost together inside one bamboo internode.

The Leopard Cat *right* does not specifically live in the bamboo, but is an opportunist, hunting wherever small prey is likely to be found.

On the Rocks

Rocky areas are often rather barren, devoid of much in the way of vegetation except lichens, ferns and a few scrubby succulents. They may also be inhospitably hot by day and cold by night. However, their great advantage is the refuge they offer to small animals that can creep beneath and among them, to escape both enemies and temperature extremes.

The Spectacled Elephant Shrew *top left* jumps along on its hind legs like a bouncing rubber ball. It feeds on insects and sleeps in rock crevices. The one or two babies are large and well-developed at birth, like those of guinea pigs or spiny mice. Elephant shrews often sunbathe on the warm rocks.

Spiny Mice *bottom left* also like to sunbathe, and will do so in a family cluster. These mice often match the colour of the rocks among which they live; in an area of purple-grey rocks they have grey fur.

The Rock Hyrax *top right* emerges from among the boulders at dawn and awaits the sun's warmth. This curious rabbit-sized animal, the coney of the Bible, looks like a rodent, but its nearest relatives are the giant pachyderms – elephant, rhinoceros and hippo. There are two kinds of hyraxes. The Rock Hyrax lives in colonies on cliffs and rocky outcrops, feeding on leaves and grasses while keeping a sharp lookout for pythons, leopards or eagles. The nocturnal Tree Hyrax lives in forest trees.

The Chinchilla *bottom right* is a relative of the guinea pig, renowned for its very soft fur. In the wild it has been so hunted for its fur that it now survives only in remote rocky areas in the High Andes. As well as a sun-bath, the chinchilla also enjoys a dust bath, rolling in dry sand.

49

Small Meat-eaters

The smallest mongoose is the Dwarf Mongoose *top left*. This is so small that it can easily fit down the underground ventilation shafts excavated by termites. Parties of these little mongooses hunt together feeding on termites as well as on other insects, and on birds' eggs, small snakes and so on. They keep in touch with each other with little bird-like calls.

The Stoat *right* is about the same size as the Dwarf Mongoose, and about as inquisitive, but is a solitary animal except when a female takes her troop of babies out hunting. This is a notoriously blood-thirsty creature, but it has to be; small mammals are its food and it must kill to eat. In the winter the stoats living in the north turn white as camouflage in the snow–all except the end of the tail, which remains black. They are then known as Ermine *bottom left*.

The Hedgehog

The European Hedgehog is one of the best-loved garden animals; no other wild animal has food so frequently put out for it. It relishes bread-and-milk, although its normal diet is slugs and snails, insects, worms, frogs, mice, birds' eggs and even snakes. At twilight it comes out to forage, in woodlands, fields and parks as well as gardens *right*. It is rarely seen by day, being then tucked up asleep somewhere in a nest of dead leaves.

Two of the most remarkable things about a hedgehog are its coat of prickles and its habit of rolling itself up into a spiky ball *top left*. When slightly disturbed, a hedgehog's first reaction is to tuck its nose down and raise its spines; only when prodded does it curl right up into a ball. This is a very effective defence against a natural enemy such as a fox, which will probably prick its nose and paws the first time it meets a hedgehog and leave them alone thereafter. However, a badger can unroll and kill a hedgehog, and the prickle-raising is no defence against that unnatural predator, the motor car.

Another remarkable thing about the hedgehog is a curious habit known as 'self-anointing'. Sometimes a hedgehog will chew and lick at something until it has worked up a mouthful of foamy saliva; then it braces itself with legs apart, leans round as far as it can reach, and repeatedly flicks the foam onto its prickles with its surprisingly big tongue *bottom left*. It may go on chewing and spitting for half an hour or more, until its flanks and neck are covered with foam, after which it totters off exhausted. There is as yet no satisfactory explanation for the behaviour. It has little to do with getting rid of fleas, but appears more like a person dabbing on scent or after-shave. Some hedgehogs never seem to get the habit while other are compulsive self-anointers.

During winter hedgehogs hibernate in a large leaf-and-moss nest. While deeply asleep, the body temperature and pulse rate drop, and the animal hardly seems to breathe. What nourishment its body needs is supplied by special fat deposits accumulated during the previous summer and autumn; these rapidly produce heat when the temperature of the surrounding air drops, so that the hedgehog in effect sleeps wrapped in a thermostatically-controlled blanket.

Nest Babies

Baby House Mice are born after a short gestation of about 20 days; they are blind, naked and deaf at birth and a dark pink *top left*. Their fur soon begins to grow as fine silky down and by seven days *top centre* they are quite well furred and more active within the nest, sleeping most of the time when not feeding, but also grooming themselves and vying with each other for warmest place in the heap. By fifteen days *bottom left* their eyes are almost opening and they are well furred. Three days later their beady eyes will be wide and they will be leaving the nest experimentally. Five weeks after weaning they themselves will begin to breed. Since each mother may have 5 or 6 babies at a time and 6-10 litters a year, populations can increase explosively. Pet mice, too, such as these ruby-eyed greys, domesticated House Mice, can quickly reproduce in the same explosive manner.

Precocious Babies

Most kinds of small rodents, as well as small insectivores and meat-eaters, are born in an early stage of development, but a few species give birth to well developed young, with eyes open, capable of running within an hour of birth. Guinea Pigs, for instance, have a rather long gestation of about 68 days, and the two to six babies are well furred, grooming themselves before they are even dry *top right*. Soon they follow their mothers onto warm rocks to bask *bottom right*. At only one day old they start to nibble solid food. At three weeks they are weaned, but females do not begin breeding until two months old, so, as rodents go, their rate of reproduction is not very high. Some other small mammals which produce precocial young are hares, spiny mice, hyraxes and elephant shrews.

Brown Rats

The names 'brown rat' and 'black rat' can cause confusion because both kinds of rats vary in colour. The 'brown rat' is usually brown *left* but it can be black, so now it is called the Common Rat. The 'black rat' is often brown *right centre* so now is called the Ship Rat. A brown Common Rat can be distinguished from a brown Ship Rat by its smaller ears, coarser fur and shorter, stouter tail. The Common Rat prefers cellars, sewers and farm buildings, whereas the Ship Rat is a great climber and lives in attics.

The white rats used in laboratories are specially bred albino Common Rats. The history of how they came to be domesticated has been lost, but they are very docile and besides being invaluable experimental animals also make affectionate and intelligent pets *bottom right*. Pet rats have also been bred in a variety of colours such as the Black-hooded *top right*.

Albinos

In the wild, an albino is a one-in-a-million animal. There is always the chance of it turning up, but it is extremely rare and nobody knows why one should suddenly appear when it does, or what the effect of its whiteness may be on it. Albinos are individuals that lack all colour pigment in fur and skin, so that the fur appears pure white and the skin pink.

In the wild, a white individual is at a great disadvantage, since against a normal background it stands out far too distinctly. The normal colour of the Mongolian Gerbil *top left* is sandy with a white belly; among granite pebbles or a gravelly terrain it merges with its surrounding. Only in the snow is an albino at an advantage over its normal mates.

Albinos are very often favoured as pets because they are more docile than those with the dark colouring. For instance, rabbits of some domesticated breeds, particularly black or piebald, can be quite fierce, whereas albinos tend to be gentle and make better pets for children. An albino Rabbit *right* may turn up among a population of wild rabbits due to an escaped pet interbreeding with the wild bunnies.

Among domesticated animals, albinos tend to be quite common, and some strains always breed true to the albino colouring. The eyes of an albino such as the Guinea Pig *bottom left* are dark pink because the red cells in the blood vessels at the back of the eyes are not masked by any dark pigment, as they are in coloured individuals. Guinea Pigs were first domesticated by the Incas, although it is not certain which species of wild guinea pig they came from, nor how they were brought to Europe and so spread around the world. The name 'guinea' probably means 'foreign'.

Sleepers

All dormice are nocturnal. By day they curl up to sleep in a small spherical nest of leaves or shredded creeper bark, in a hollow tree or in the ground, and are not easily awakened. Unlike most small mammals that seem to sleep with one eye open and are ready to leap out of their nest at the least alarm, the dormouse resents being disturbed in the daytime and stays profoundly asleep. If shaken awake like the Dormouse at the Mad Hatter's teaparty, it is grumpy and bad-tempered. In addition, dormice that live in northern latitudes hibernate for half the year. In autumn their daily sleep lasts longer and longer until in October they fail to wake at all for the night. During hibernation they stay tightly curled up and can be rolled about without waking. They do not rouse themselves until April. While thus asleep the body temperature and heart rate drop so that the animal is hardly breathing, in a state of suspended animation. What little energy it needs comes from the layers of fat put on in the autumn, and the dormouse may lose half its body weight by the spring. Dormice, such as the African Dormouse, that live in tropical forests, do not of course hibernate.

The Garden Dormouse of Europe *left* has a black tufted tail and a black eye-mark which makes its eyes look even bigger. It spends more time on the ground than do other dormice, and may even live among rocks rather than bushes.

The favourite food of the Hazel Dormouse *top right* is hazel nuts. Where other mice lay in winter stores of nuts or other goodies, the dormouse eats most of its nuts and accumulates stores of fat to tide it over the winter.

The very name dormouse comes from the Latin verb meaning to sleep. The Hazel Dormouse *bottom right* sleeps through the winter in a leaf nest, tightly curled with its paws bunched and its tail wrapped around it. The neat holes it gnaws in hazel nuts are characteristic; Long-tailed Field Mice gnaw irregular holes and squirrels split the shells.

Activity

Small mammals, when not actually asleep, seem to have boundless energy, and sometimes one wonders where it comes from when all they eat is a few seeds. With such energy to use up, it is not very kind to confine an animal to a small bare cage with nothing for it to do except sleep and eat and tidy up its fur.

An activity wheel *top left* is a well-tried toy for cage-bound animals. It is obvious from the amount of time pet mice spend on or in it, that it fulfils a need. But it is not only pet mice and other domesticated small animals that enjoy a wheel. Scientific studies have been carried out on all kinds of animals from wolves to weasels and squirrels to harvest mice and all have been found to enjoy and benefit from the exercise. Caged animals that do not have to hunt or forage for their own food have a lot of time and energy to use up. Unfortunately, the wheels one can buy for small pets are far from satisfactory; they are usually flimsily built and far too small for a rat or hamster when the animals are full grown. Some bought wheels are made of thin wire bars; small climbing mice such as Long-tails or Deer Mice enjoy these because their feet are adept at finding holds among twigs, but voles, gerbils and hamsters do not like them—their feet keep falling through the bars. A very good solid wheel can be made out of a round biscuit tin minus its lid, with a spindle for the wheel to turn on. A mouse or hamster does not seem to mind how large a wheel it has, so long as it turns easily, but it will not use a too-small wheel that bends its back the wrong way. Devising and making a suitable wheel for a pet can be as much fun and satisfaction for the owner as for the animal.

The Golden Hamster is not built for jumping and climbing; its table-like construction of a short leg at each corner of a rectangular body suits it for running rapidly along the ground. It is surprising therefore how much time a bored hamster will spend swinging by its hands from the bars of its cage-top *bottom left* like a clumsily-brachiating gibbon. With a wheel to trundle, this same hamster will not need this uncomfortable-looking form of exercise. However, it can happen that a pet hamster, given a nice large wheel, hardly seems to use it, and this can be disappointing when much time and thought have gone into the construction. In fact the animal may be turning the wheel most of the night, since the disadvantage of a hamster is its nocturnal habits. One way to find out is to fit the wheel with a counter such as a cycle milometer, with a ratchet so that the wheel can be turned in one direction only. A family of Zebra Mice *top right* clocked up the equivalent of a journey of twenty miles in a week, either running inside the wheel or standing outside and turning with three feet. This does not mean that in the wild Zebra Mice would run at random over this sort of distance. Most small mammals are quite restricted in their movements, each individual staying within its small home range and only leaving it under exceptional circumstances.

The pet Common Genet *bottom right* could well have benefited from a wheel to turn, but to avert boredom it was allowed out of its cage whenever possible to roam and explore the rest of the house. Genets in the wild feed on any other small animal they can catch, so a goldfish in a bowl aroused Jenny's hunting instincts. Like a cat, a genet is not fond of water, and the goldfish frequently got its own back by splashing the genet, an accidental stratagem perhaps, but one that caused the genet to look for something interesting elsewhere.

63

INDEX

Photographs supplied by:
Bruce Coleman Ltd., 16a-17a Windsor Street, Uxbridge, Middlesex, England.